Whilst it is likely that Frederick and George Lanchester built the first full-scale four-wheeled petrol car of truly British origin to run in Great Britain, John Henry Knight of Farnham is thought to have run the first British-made vehicle on public roads. The Knight car seen here was built in 1895 as a three-wheeler and very soon converted to four wheels to gain stability. The simple spoon brake against the rear tyre is clearly seen, as is the crude form of independent front suspension. It is obvious that Knight was having trouble keeping the tyres of the front wheels on the rim; they were held on with rope.

VETERAN MOTOR CARS

Michael E. Ware

Shire Publications Ltd

CONTENTS

Published in 2003 by Shire Publications Ltd, Cromwell House, Church Street, Princes Risborough, Buckinghamshire HP27 9AA, UK. Website: www.shirebooks.co.uk Copyright © 1983 by Michael E. Ware. First published 1983; reprinted 1987 and 2003. Shire Album 112. ISBN 0 85263 658 X.

Printed in Great Britain by CIT Printing Services Ltd, Press Buildings, Merlins Bridge, Haverfordwest, Pembrokeshire SA61 1XF.

AUTHOR'S NOTE

The Veteran Car Club of Great Britain caters for cars built up to and in 1918. In general terms, therefore, all cars of this period are known as Veterans, but those vehicles built after 1904 and before 1919 are often referred to as Edwardian, although these dates do not cover the Edwardian period exactly.

Though motor cars developed independently in the United States, Europe and Great Britain, this book concentrates on the early years of the motor car in Great Britain.

ACKNOWLEDGEMENTS

For the first edition of this book I received great help from colleagues at the National Motor Museum, particularly Peter Brockes (Librarian), Philip Scott (Photographic Librarian), David Miller (Photographer) and the late Howard Wilson (Chief Engineer). I am very grateful to the late Michael Sedgwick for reading the manuscript and making many useful comments. June Slater and my wife, Janet, typed the manuscript and I am most grateful to both of them for their great help.

All the photographs reproduced in this book come from the files of the Photographic Library, National Motor Museum, Beaulieu.

Cover: *There are eleven years between the two cars shown: a 1901 English-built Progress and an importation from Italy, the 1913 Fiat. Both are typical cheap owner-driver cars of the veteran period. Both have been designed to carry four people. The motor car developed very fast in its formative years.*

TO MOTORISTS.

Please DRIVE SLOWLY so as not to SMOTHER the growing Crops with DUST.

From 1865 to 1878 the law stated that a man holding a red flag had to walk 60 yards (55 m) in front of all self-propelled locomotives on the public highway. This picture taken in 1869 shows a Tasker self-propelled traction engine going from the makers at Andover to an agricultural show in Southampton. It is a posed photograph and the man is not 60 yards in front, but it is quite likely that it is the only genuine picture in existence taken during the period when the red flag was obligatory.

THE NINETEENTH CENTURY

Each year some three hundred owners of pre-1905 cars gather in Hyde Park, London, on the first Sunday in November for a fifty mile drive to the seaside at Brighton. It is estimated that they are watched by over a million people spread along the route, and the enthusiasm of the spectators is tremendous. Originally looked upon as something of a joke, this event is now a national institution known as the London to Brighton Veteran Car Run (or just the 'Brighton Run') and has been held almost without a break (the Second World War apart) since 1927.

What, therefore, is the tradition of this event, and why is it so important in motoring history? It dates back to the Emancipation Run of 1896, but, in order to understand that, we must look briefly at some of the laws which governed the

use of a self-propelled vehicle on the roads of Great Britain during the nineteenth century.

The development of the self-propelled traction engine, the passenger carrying steam carriage, and latterly the motor vehicle (referred to as a light locomotive) was stifled by completely unrealistic laws. The Locomotive Act of 1861 fixed a maximum speed on the open road of 10 miles (16 km) an hour and required that a self-propelled steam vehicle be conducted by two persons. This was quite reasonable, but very quickly a number of rival factions, including the railways, had the laws changed and in 1865 Parliament passed the so-called 'Red Flag Act', which required that 'at least three persons shall be employed to drive or conduct such a locomotive . . . one such

Saturday 14th November 1896 – motor cars were now allowed to travel on the public highway for the first time without being preceded by a man 'walking in front'. The Motor Car Club organised the Emancipation Run from London to Brighton to celebrate this occasion, and this photograph shows one of the two American Duryea cars en route to Brighton. The event was so badly organised that we do not know which car got to Brighton first, but a statement sworn before a commissioner of oaths by a passenger on one of the Duryeas claimed that it was the first to arrive.

person . . shall precede each locomotive on foot by not less than 60 yards (55 m) carrying a red flag constantly on display.' The same Act lowered the speed limit to 4 miles (6.4 km) per hour. In 1878 the Highways and Locomotive Amendment Act repealed the need for a red flag, but still required the third man to precede the locomotive by at least 20 yards (18 m).

On the continent of Europe Benz had built his first car in 1885 and had been followed the next year by Daimler, thus making the two German firms Europe's first motor vehicle manufacturers, but the first full scale four-wheeled petrol car of truly British origin was designed by Frederick and George Lanchester in 1894 and completed in 1896. Britain lagged behind the continent for two reasons. Since the death of the Prince Consort in 1861, there was no enthusiastic leadership from the Royal Family, Queen Victoria having gone into seclusion, and this attitude was reflected by Parliament. Britain also lagged behind the continent because the laws relating to the self-propelled vehicle on the roads were so restrictive.

In November 1896 the law was changed. The need for a man walking in front was abolished, and the speed limit was raised to 12 miles (19 km) an hour. To celebrate this freedom of the road, the newly formed Motor Car Club organised a run from London to Brighton on Saturday 14th November, the day on which the new law came into force.

The first imports into Britain of continental cars that can be traced occurred in 1895, and so by November 1896 there could have been only seventy or eighty motor vehicles in Britain. Therefore an entry of over fifty-four before the London to Brighton run was quite an achievement, although only thirty-three actually started the drive.

The Motor Car Club was controlled by H. J. Lawson, who had bought a number of foreign patents relating to the motor vehicle, and he formed motor manufacturing companies to work the patents under licence. The first of these, and by

4

far the best, was the Daimler Motor Company, promoted by him before the Act was repealed. The Emancipation Run was very much a publicity stunt for those manufacturers associated with Lawson. The run itself was extremely badly organised, and to this day it is not certain which was the first car to arrive at Brighton. Considering the importance now attached to that event, it is a pity it was so chaotic. On the other hand, it did receive wide mention in the press and, though the reports are at times contradictory, they did for the first time spread throughout Britain the news of the arrival of the motor car as a serious means of transport. But to show how far Britain was behind the continent, in June 1895 France held a motor race from Paris to Bordeaux and back, a distance of 732 miles (1178 km), which was won by Emile Levassor driving a Panhard-Levassor at an average speed of 15 miles (24 km) an hour.

It is not surprising, therefore, that the first cars seen in any quantity on the public roads in Britain were imported from the continent. The principal makes were Benz, Panhard-Levassor and Peugeot. During the last four years of the century the British motor industry, led by Daimler, tried to catch up.

On the Sunday after their arrival at Brighton, the cars gave a demonstration run up and down the sea front. This is one of a series of well known photographs taken outside the Hotel Metropole on that occasion and shows Mr A. Cornell of Tonbridge at the wheel of a 3½ horsepower Benz. The lady is Mrs Bazalgette, a pioneer lady motorist and one of the first ever lady drivers. The dented tank on the front is the header tank for the radiator.

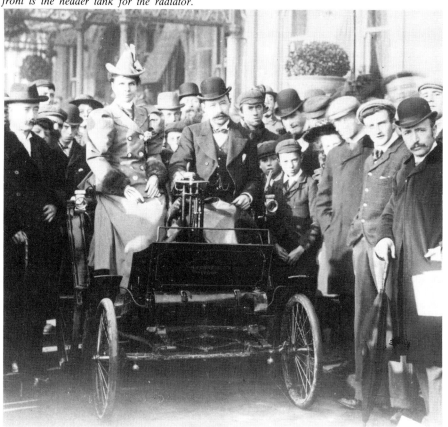

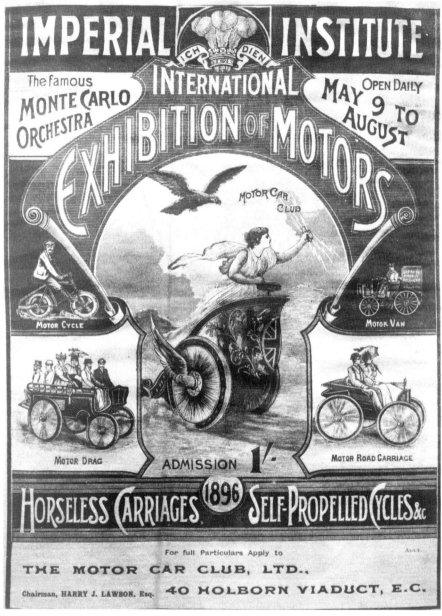

May 9th 1896 was the opening day of the summer season at the Imperial Institute, and the Prince of Wales paid an informal visit. Each year special attractions appropriate to the occasion were added to the ordinary collections of curiosities at the Institute. In 1896 horseless carriages were the attraction.

This Benz dog cart of c 1900 follows horse-drawn practice very closely. On some models the passengers sat behind the driver, facing to the rear, but on this particular car the box at the front has been built up, and passengers would sit facing the driver, and presumably block his view. This illustration comes from a postcard which must be dated 1905 or later; it is certainly after the coming of the Act requiring vehicles to have registration numbers, which came into force at the beginning of 1904. Even so, the postcard manufacturer has captioned the picture 'The old and the new'. This gives some idea how unusual, in some places, the sight of a motor car could still be.

MAKING VICTORIAN CARS WORK

Early cars were uncomfortable, very noisy, slow, smelly and afflicted with bad brakes. Inventors concentrated on fitting their experimental engines into formerly horse-propelled vehicles (hence the term 'horseless carriage'). Engines were hung wherever convenient to make a conventional horse-drawn vehicle mobile under its own power. They even used the same names for bodywork: wagonette, dog cart and phaeton, for example. As the motor car became more refined, so a specially constructed chassis was required, but even then the influence of the horse-drawn vehicle was to linger for many years.

Unless one could afford a private carriage, road transport was by the spartan horse bus or the unprotected vehicles of local carriers. The first motorists therefore accepted the lack of protection and the crudity of their vehicles as a matter of course and dressed accordingly.

Panhard and Levassor in 1891 were the first to put together what became for many years the accepted layout for cars, with a vertically mounted engine in front of the driver, giving weight where it would help the adhesion of the wheels which did the steering. The Panhard had a friction clutch and a form of gearbox, at first with chain drive to the back axle, a system which gradually gave way to shaft drive to a differential.

Most horse-drawn vehicles had no chassis and could support only a light engine. Soon a chassis or frame was incorporated, made of wood, or wood with steel strengthening plates. Some light cars had a tubular frame based on bicycle practice, but early in the twentieth century the rigid pressed steel chassis became common, especially where a degree of series production was adopted.

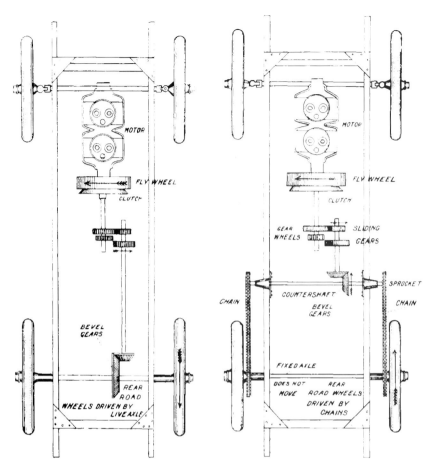

THE LIVE AXLE, OR CARDAN DRIVE.

The drive is from the motor crank-shaft on to the fly-wheel, through the clutch to the fixed gears. The engaging of the fixed and sliding-gears conveys the power on to the cardan or propeller shaft, and the bevel-gears at the end of this shaft turn the power at right angles on to the live-axle, which is fixed to the road-wheels. The differential is not shown.

THE DRIVE THROUGH SIDE-CHAINS.

In this type the power is taken in the same way, through the clutch to the fixed and sliding-gears. It is turned at right angles through bevel-gears on to the counter-shaft. At either end of this are fixed the chain-sprockets, which drive the road-wheels through side-chains. The axle in this case does not revolve. The arrows in each diagram show the direction of rotation.

The two types of transmission in motor cars: a rough simplified plan showing the two methods of drive.

8

Solid tyres together with crude suspension gave a very hard ride. Even though pneumatics still had serious problems, they proved to be more popular. Punctures were commonplace, and all motorists would have to know how to change or repair a tube at the roadside. Here, Mrs Kennard of Market Harborough, a very keen motorist, receives instruction from the family chauffeurs on the various ways of repairing a puncture.

The flexing of these chassis was incompatible with the simple suspension of horse carriages, and bodywork fractures were frequent. Axles and wheels were simple; the wooden wheel was capable of taking the extra speed and side forces of the earliest cars. The bicycle industry had pioneered the spoked wheel, but spokes were arranged radially and thus would not always withstand sudden changes of direction. Lanchester was the first firm to use wheels spoked tangentially, that is to say, with the spokes overlapping. This arrangement soon won general acceptance.

Tyres were one of the greatest problems for the earliest motorist, and though Michelin had used pneumatic tyres in the Paris-Bordeaux-Paris race of 1895, most cars used solid rubber tyres until the high pressure beaded-edge type became more reliable at the end of the century. This was expensive to buy and was damaged

and punctured easily. Roads were mainly unmetalled; surfaces contained many sharp flints, and hobnails dropped from the shoes of horses were a constant hazard.

Braking on horse-drawn vehicles was very poor. The spoon brake pressing on the tyre was as unsuitable for cars as it had been for dog carts. The simplest car brake was a block which pressed on to the transmission countershaft. The external contracting block brake was popular before 1900; in this system a number of blocks of wood were attached to a steel rope which ran round a special ring attached to the hub. One end of the rope was fixed, and the brakes worked as pressure pulled the rope tight. To stop a car from running away backwards, a hinged pointed sprag could be lowered at the rear in the hope that this would stop progress. In some extreme cases, the car leap-frogged over its sprag and continued

External Contracting Brake.

Internal Expanding Brake.

ABOVE: *In February 1899 Edwin Sewell and his passenger were killed in Britain's first fatal motor accident. While descending a steep hill in Harrow, the Daimler's normally ineffectual brakes suddenly jammed; the force pulled the spokes of the rear wheels out of the rim, and the driver and passenger were thrown out of the car. Whilst wooden wheels, hardly any different from those on horse-drawn vehicles, could withstand many of the pressures put on them by the motor car, a sudden change in impetus could cause damage such as this.*

LEFT: *The earlier type of braking was the external contracting brake, where a lined metal band was pulled on to the hub. One of the chief disadvantages of this system was that if the hub and the brake got wet, the braking efficiency was greatly impaired. Later came the internal expanding brake, where two shoes, each fitted with a special lining, were forced outwards against a drum. This was much more efficient and the drum itself gave considerable protection against the weather.*

on its errant way! Later, contracting band brakes replaced the blocks of wood, but fortunately the drum brake (still in use today) appeared as early as 1901.

Various forms of steam engine had been in use for years, as had the oil engine, which was powered by ordinary lighting oils such as kerosene or paraffin marketed under such names as Royal Daylight, Water White or Russoline. Gas

10

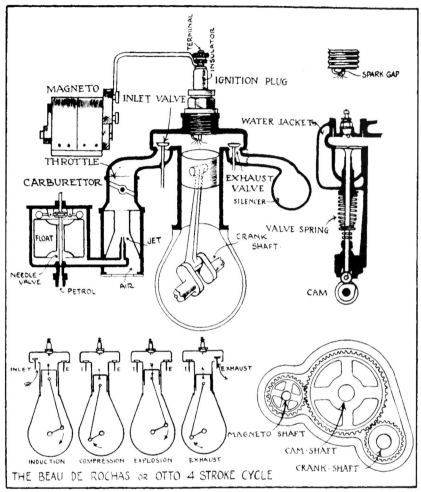

Diagrammatic drawing illustrating the elements of a petrol engine. The piston, connecting rod and crankshaft are shown in perspective in a cylinder that is shown in section. Below is a series of diagrams illustrating the four strokes of the Otto cycle. During the suction stroke, the descending piston acts as the plunger of an air-pump to draw air from the atmosphere past the throttle valve and the inlet valve into the cylinder. Flowing through the contracted choke-tube surrounding the jet of the carburettor, the air causes petrol to spray therefrom and thus becomes carburetted with its vapour. The mixture thus formed is explosive when compressed by the return stroke of the piston. As the piston reaches the top of its compression stroke, a spark occurs at the ignition plug, thus starting combustion in the gaseous mixture. Combustion is propagated through the gas so quickly as to cause explosion, and the consequent rise in temperature results in expansion of the burning gas, and also of the inert nitrogen of the air, which does not enter into the combustion. The piston is thus driven to the bottom of the cylinder and performs the one working stroke of the cycle. During the return stroke, the burnt gases are expelled through the exhaust valve into the silencer. The valves are generally mechanically opened by cams mounted on a shaft that is gear-driven from the crankshaft. The closing of the valve is effected by a spring.

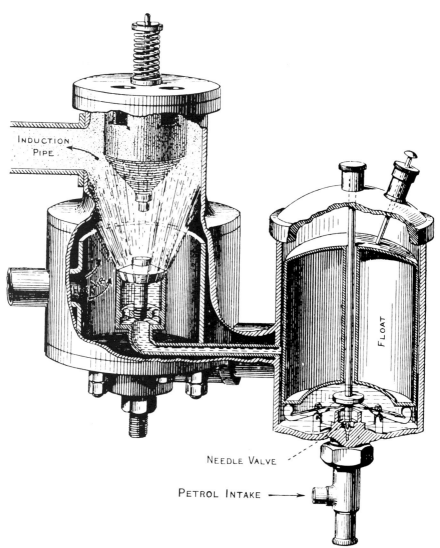

INDUCTION PIPE

FLOAT

NEEDLE VALVE

PETROL INTAKE →

A Simple Type of Automatic Carburettor.

The speed of a car is governed by the amount of petrol passing through the carburettor. Petrol flows past the needle valve, which shuts off when the level is sufficient to lift the float off the two levers on which it sits. When the piston in the engine is on the induction stroke, petrol is drawn through the jet along with a measured supply of air, and the petrol is atomised into a mixture which passes into the cylinder for combustion.

ABOVE: *It is reputed that the first motor car to be seen in Scotland was imported by Tom Elliot in December 1895. He is seen here standing beside the car, an 1895 3½ horsepower Panhard. Note the very simple iron-shod wooden wheels, the impressive-looking but inefficient candle lamps, and the tiller steering. The front doors of the engine compartment being open, we can see the burner box for the hot tube ignition system.*

RIGHT: *In order to transmit the power from the engine to the rear axle, it was necessary to have some form of clutch which could be depressed, so switching off the power to the drive, but keeping the engine running. The cone clutch operating within the flywheel was the first and most simple form. The cone was usually faced with leather engaging with a metal surface. Often in the earlier vehicles this clutch was very fierce and had to be treated liberally with neatsfoot oil to make it slip a little. This was followed later by the single-plate clutch where pressure was applied against friction discs, not the outer housing.*

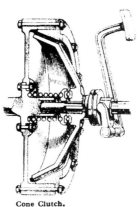

Cone Clutch.

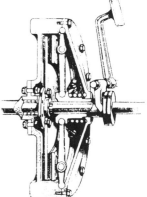

Single Plate Clutch.

13

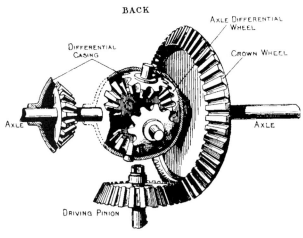

BACK

AXLE DIFFERENTIAL WHEEL

DIFFERENTIAL CASING

CROWN WHEEL

AXLE

AXLE

DRIVING PINION

FRONT

A Half-perspective Drawing of a Differential.

From the earliest time it was realised that some form of differential gear was required in the rear axle of the car, that is to say, a gearing which allowed the inside wheel to turn more slowly relative to the outside wheel as the car was going round a corner. Without a differential the inside wheel would scuff and the tyre would wear out extremely quickly.

oil and benzoline were classed as petroleum and had not been used very much for stationary engines. The first car engines were developed from the oil engine and seldom had more than one cylinder. These units were capable of only a few hundred revolutions per minute, compared with five thousand or even more on the motor cars of today.

It was the German engineer Nikolaus August Otto who built the first four-stroke engine; he used the four strokes of the piston and two revolutions of the crankshaft to achieve this. On the first stroke, the air and the petrol are sucked into the cylinder; on the second stroke the air and the petrol are compressed; on the third stroke the mixture is fired and pushed down the piston, and on the fourth stroke the burnt petrol is exhausted. In order to achieve a proper air/petrol mixture, it is necessary for the latter to be in vaporised form. The earliest equipment to achieve this was called a 'surface carburettor', air being drawn over a large open pan of petrol. In later designs the air was passed over a wick heavily soaked in petrol. The spray carburettor which is in general use today can be traced back to the early part of the twentieth century.

To achieve the explosion, red heat or a spark is required. The first ignition systems worked on the 'hot tube' principle. A platinum tube was inserted into a recess in the cylinder head, and this tube was maintained at red heat by a petrol or spirit burner on the outside. Each time the piston arrived at the top of the compression stroke, so a little of the mixture was forced into the recess containing the red hot tube and the resultant flashback ignited the main body of the petrol inside the cylinder. Later the electrical magneto became commonplace, a machine identical in action to the medical shocking coil. The impulses of the magneto are distributed to ignition (sparking) plugs fitted into the cylinder. When the impulse is delivered, a very hot electric spark jumps between the points of the plug, so igniting the petrol.

To stop overheating, most engines were water-jacketed. At first large quantities of water were carried in containers out in front in the airstream. The quantity of water, as much as the action of the passing air, kept temperatures down. It was not long before the radiator came into being. Here, numerous small tubes were connected to cool the hot water. To help dissipate the heat more easily, a great number of small fins were attached to the tubes. Later the water pump became commonplace to circulate the hot water more quickly through the cooling fins and the tubes.

The steam car was popular for a few years, particularly the lighter Locomobiles and Stanleys. Steam cars were imported from America, and this 1900 Locomobile has been used for a publicity stunt. Hubert Egerton drove the car 880 miles (1416 km) from John O'Groats to Lands End with apparently very little trouble. Stunts of this sort were very popular in the early days of motoring.

THE EDWARDIAN ERA

By 1905 the car was beginning to have a shape of its own. One of the most popular body styles to emerge in the early 1900s was the rear-entrance tonneau. Here the rear seats ran around the sides of the body, facing inwards. The door was therefore in the rear. It was difficult to fit a satisfactory hood to this body, and it gradually went out of favour. However, there was still a tendency to hang things on the outside of the car, which gave the impression of a lack of cohesion of design; this is strange when compared with the great attention to detail to be seen in every minor part.

As cars went faster, better weather protection and greater comfort were required even on the cheaper models. There were very few closed bodies before 1906. Such styles were heavy, and many early cars were underpowered; they were also much more expensive to manufac-ture. The closed car was used principally on formal occasions; it had to cater for ladies with flowing dresses and large hats, as well as tall gentlemen wearing their top hats, who needed to step into their limousines without undue stooping. This resulted in very high cars, often top-heavy in appearance. The first popular type of closed car was the landaulette, a body style on which the rear part of the heavy leather top folded right down so that in good weather the occupants could take the air.

Cars were available from manufactur-ers in either chassis form or, less fre-quently, with a factory-made body. If you bought the former you took the chassis to the coachbuilder, who then built a body to your own specification. By contrast, factory coachwork was of standard type and batch production kept prices down. Mass production, however, did not reach

This 1906 Renault limousine is typical of the early closed car of the Edwardian period. The history of the car shows that the interior was modelled on that of a French first-class railway carriage, the original owner specifying that he could get into the car whilst wearing his top hat. The wide flared wings — to keep the dust out — are clearly shown. This car is fitted with the Stepney rim, which could be affixed alongside a punctured tyre.

Britain until 1911, when a Model T Ford production line was set up at Trafford Park in Manchester. It was not until well after the period of this book that closed bodies became common on mass-produced cars.

The standard of finish achieved by the Edwardian coachbuilders was very high and followed the standard set by the makers of horse-drawn carriages. Some forty applications of paint, sealer, primer, undercoat and varnish were commonplace. The result had a gloss finish of marvellous depth.

A prominent feature on any car was the mudguarding. Originally mudguards were insubstantial, often made of bent-wood, but in attempts to keep road dust out of the car they soon became very much wider, with attractive curves and flares. The floor of an Edwardian car was relatively high, necessitating a step, which gradually became bigger. Eventually it joined the two wings, to become known as the running board, a feature which persisted until the Second World War. On to this running board were fitted tool boxes, battery boxes, acetylene generators, spare tins of petrol, spare wheels and even luggage, except on a landaulette, where it was often stowed on the roof, kept in place by a neat brass roof rail.

As road speeds increased, so lighting had to be improved. Acetylene lamps grew bigger and more powerful, but after

ABOVE: *Five ladies dressed up to go motoring, their hats held on by scarves, and their knees covered by a heavy rug. The lack of doors at the front was one of the reasons why it was necessary to keep the knees covered. In order that some hand luggage and other small objects could be carried, this car is fitted with a wicker basket around the rear part of the bodywork, a common accessory of the day. The bodywork is the popular rear entrance tonneau type. The car is a 1903 Clement and is fitted with a good pair of acetylene headlamps and a magnificent and powerful spotlight.*

BELOW: *In many Napiers, the radiator was placed forward of the front axle, giving them an ungainly appearance. This saloon, with a body by the famous firm of Mulliner of Northampton, has a very high floor because of its side-chain drive. Inside, at the rear, can be seen one of the occasional seats, which swings into place once the door is closed. Each body turned out by a coachbuilder was different from the previous one. They were individually photographed, and many albums of these pictures survive to show the fascinating art of Edwardian special bodywork.*

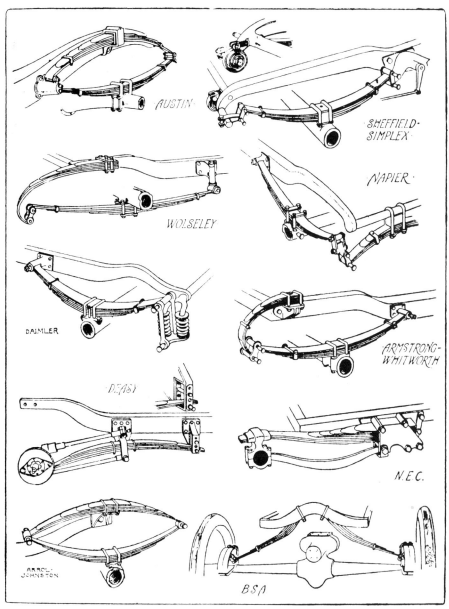

Because the tyres were run at a very high pressure, often between 40 and 100 pounds (18-45 kg), the ride experienced by the occupants was often very hard indeed. In order to give the passengers a more comfortable ride, various types and combinations of springing were tried, all being variants of the old-fashioned cart spring.

The best of the lightweight cyclecars was the Morgan, first built in 1910 at a factory at Malvern Link. Better constructed than most, the Morgan has weathered many storms and still survives. This well used early example is, unusually, equipped with electric headlamps and an exhaust-operated whistle mounted straight off the exhaust manifold.

each trip the spent carbide had to be emptied. Electric lighting was slowly coming in, but recharging batteries was difficult as the dynamo was not efficient at all speeds. The lights tended to take more out of the battery than the dynamo put in.

Tyres were still a problem, but as roads improved so did tyre design. Advances were made in dealing with punctures, a constant hazard. First came the Stepney rim, which could be bolted on to the punctured wheel and used as a get-you-home device. Soon the rims themselves became detachable, so that the offending tyre or tube could easily be taken from the wheel and a new one put on. The wheels themselves were still non-detachable. Then the Rudge-Whitworth style became available, a wheel whose hub contained a number of splines held in place by a single nut tightened by blows of a hammer or a special spanner. Many cars still carried at least two spare wheels, rims, tyres or tubes.

Engines developed only as foundry techniques and the knowledge of metallurgy improved. They became very much neater, being integrally designed rather than lumps of metal with a lot of ancillaries hung on them. All Edwardian engines were, by modern standards, low revving and lightly stressed. They were, as a result, very long lasting. Even at the end of the period the individual cylinders were not water-jacketed, only their heads. Progress was made in radiator design and many varied shapes appeared, even round ones on cars such as the Bentall or Delaunay-Belleville, the latter firm supposedly choosing the shape as it was better known for its marine boilers.

Starting the car was always an inconvenience. The only way to start the engine was to crank it with a starting handle, often a heavy and wearisome process. If the mixture and the ignition were not quite right, it took a long time. If the ignition had not been retarded properly, the car could backfire, breaking the driver's arm or wrist. The owner-driver wanted an easier system, while lady motorists could only cope with the smallest of light cars. Late in the period, compressed air starters had some success, but it was not until 1912 that one could buy a car with full dynamo electric lighting and starting — the American Cadillac. By 1914 most of the more expensive British cars could be bought with electric starting.

Brakes improved, but not as rapidly as the speed and weight of cars increased. Usually the footbrake worked on the transmission and was used more in emergencies than for anything else, as it tended to put a great strain on the propeller shaft, the gearbox and the back

axle if liberally applied. The handbrake worked the drums on the rear wheels only. Front wheel brakes were not commonplace until the 1920s.

It is easy to get the impression that all cars of this period were large, but this is not so. There were always a few makers trying to bridge the gap between the motorcycle and the car. By 1912 a new breed appeared — the cyclecar, a light tubular frame with a motorcycle engine and a light two-seater body, sometimes with tandem seating. Makes such as Morgan and AC grew up and still survive, but long gone are the Bédélia, Eric, Sabella, AV, Crouch and Wall. Some of these very crude low-price cars had all the vices of their earliest forebears.

An enormous amount of animosity was levelled against the motorist in early years. Motorists were spat upon and whipped by horsemen who claimed that the cars were noisy and smelly and frightened their animals — all quite likely true. Here, John Roberts and Sons of Bridgwater have made up an advertising vehicle in the form of a very early tiller-steered Daimler, presumably for entry in the famous Bridgwater Carnival. Simple illumination has been set up around the horse, so presumably it was for a night-time parade.

In June 1900 the Prince of Wales took delivery of the first ever car to be owned by royalty. It was a 6 horsepower Daimler Mail Phaeton. The two front seats were protected by a fairly extensive cape cart-type hood while the passengers at the back sat on a spindly seat with no overhead protection. The candle side-lamps would have given very little forward light but would have indicated the car's presence to vehicles coming the other way.

EARLY MOTORING

In 1900 the Prince of Wales had one of his first ever motor rides – in a Daimler driven by Lord Montagu of Beaulieu. In the same year he took delivery of the first royal car, a Daimler, for use at Sandringham. Within a year, two other Daimlers were in the Sandringham stable. Queen Alexandra, who liked the quiet of an electric car, drove a Columbia but later moved on to larger petrol-engined cars. It is almost impossible for us to imagine the strength of the anti-motorist lobby around 1900, but the fact that royalty took an active interest in motoring was a great boost to the movement.

We tend to think that motoring in the early days was only for the rich. Before 1900 it was a sport for the eccentric few, but gradually this changed, and whilst cars such as Rolls-Royce, Napier and Daimler were very costly, there were plenty of small imported single-cylinder cars such as the French De Dion-Bouton or the American Oldsmobile. There were three- and four-wheeled motorcycles known as tricars or quads. Soon there was a flourishing second-hand market, so that motoring came within the reach of quite a wide range of people.

Someone who could afford a horse and trap could afford a car. A 10 horsepower model, about 1904, averaged a cost of $2^{3}/4$d a mile over 7000 miles. A horse and trap, we are told, cost about 6d per mile, and these were not likely to travel 7000 miles in a year! By 1910, an 18 to 24 horsepower Austin was costing just over 3d a mile, averaging 21.17 miles per gallon in the process. A Rolls-Royce Silver Ghost, 'The Best Car in the

21

This photograph, although taken many years later than the 1911 date, shows the costs in that year of a Model T Ford car, namely £115. As today, with most makes of car, the number plates were extra at 5s. A 2 gallon (9 litre) can of petrol was 1 shilling, and a gallon (4.5 litres) of oil was 1s 2d. Engines were not as efficient as today, and oil was required very often. The Model T Ford was often the owner's first car; therefore two hours' driving tuition at 5s was very necessary.

World', cost nearly £1,000 in chassis form, whilst a De Dion-Bouton single-cylinder in 1903 cost only £200.

Early motoring gradually came to be looked upon less as a hobby and more as a serious form of transport. Those who were used to being driven in a carriage still preferred to be driven, and so the coachman was kept on and sent to one of the many motoring schools which were springing up. Car firms such as Rolls-Royce and Napier ran their own training schools. Many such establishments taught the chauffeur to be a mechanic as well as a driver. It was not unknown for a new owner to order a chauffeur to come with the car when it was delivered. Such a person would have been trained at the manufacturer's training school. The chauffeur was still very much the servant, usually sitting in the open at the wheel, whilst his passengers enjoyed closed bodywork behind him. There was usually some form of division between the chauffeur and his passengers, and many different types of communication mechanisms were used so that passengers did not have to talk to the driver! When not on

official journeys it was not uncommon for the owner of the car, if he was an enthusiast, to drive it, with the chauffeur beside him, but only in good weather. The chauffeur was useful when dealing with breakdowns en route, particularly punctures.

The car arrived in Britain at a time when the roads were in a very poor state. The turnpike trusts had kept many main roads in good repair, but the coming of the railways had done away with the lucrative stage-coach traffic. The roads deteriorated and there were relatively few miles of sealed or macadam road. In dry weather the greatest problem on these unsealed roads was dust. Motorists believed that the dust cloud which they left behind them was the principal cause of the antagonism towards motoring. During the famous One Thousand Miles' Trial of 1900, competitors had to drive over a strip of white flour and be judged on the resulting cloud. Many special devices were tried on the cars, both to cut down the dust from the car and to protect the occupants.

Early cars had little protection for the drivers and passengers – no windscreen,

ABOVE: *Motoring in the early days was a social occupation. Many motoring garden parties were held, and rallies often took place in the grounds of stately homes. Here we see a large number of cars gathered outside a Scottish baronial castle around 1904. Most of the cars are open and have tonneau-style four-seater bodywork, whilst on the very right is an Arrol-Johnston dog cart.*
BELOW: *One of the most famous motor competitions staged in the early years was the One Thousand Miles Trial of 1900. Here at a stop near Reading, a driver is seen photographed with the town's mayor. The driver is wearing typical motoring clothes of the time — a heavy fur coat and goggles. His passenger at the rear is similarly attired. Standing behind on the right is a chauffeur in garb reminiscent of a yachtsman. The uniforms of chauffeurs often resembled those of seafarers. The dust on the front of this car demonstrates the state of the roads at the time.*

The Automobile Association was set up in the first instance to try to save motorists from persecution by the police and magistrates. Suitably equipped with Norfolk jackets and cycling breeches, the first AA Cycle Scouts of 1905 patrolled the roads at weekends, warning passing motorists of the presence of police in the area. When the disc worn on the chest showed 'AA' in yellow on a white background, this indicated there were no speed traps on the road. If the reverse side, 'AA' in black on a red background, was showing, it invariably meant a police trap.

a low scuttle and low doors, or no doors at all. No one thought that because of the extra speed of the car the occupants would need greater protection from the elements. Very quickly, however, a great clothing industry was built up to provide heavy and light coats, leather jackets, breeches and gaiters. There were even chamois-skin knickers for the lady automobilist, along with fashionable long coats, and hats secured with long scarves and veils. Heavy goggles were worn by both sexes. This clothing was to protect the owners from dust and stones as much as from the wind and weather.

The Motor Car Act of 1903 (coming into force on 1st January 1904) was partly the work of John Scott-Montagu. It required every mechanical vehicle to be registered with the local authority and fitted with registration plates. It also required every driver to have a driving licence. Many motorists were very indignant about this, saying that they were now 'numbered like convicts and labelled like hackney carriages'. Also in the Act was the provision to raise the speed limit from its lowly 12 miles (19 km) an hour to 20 (32 km). The police set up speed traps, and many motor car owners were caught speeding, as most of their vehicles were capable of exceeding 20 miles an hour. In many cases the watches used by the police were inaccurate, but it did not seem to matter. Many magistrates appeared to be anti-motorists, and the fines were heavy.

By midway through the Edwardian period, touring was not unusual. Petrol was more readily available from cycle shops, chemists or even grocers. Hotels catered for car owners, having converted their stables and provided inspection pits, so often required for overnight servicing. Signposts were not common, so many touring guides or maps were soon on sale.

Touring abroad became more commonplace, and cross-Channel ferry operators soon became accustomed to craning limousines into their holds or on to their decks. Information on foreign touring was, however, sometimes lacking. In the *Motor Manual* of 1912 it is stated that 'The rule of the road in France now is to keep to the left...' Touring abroad must have had its exciting moments.

The 1901 Progress is a pretty car in imperial crimson, lined out in gold; upholstery is black. The low doors are hardly ever used; one steps over them. The small radiator is sufficient to cool the engine. Oil headlamps are intended to show your presence, rather than to show you the way. No spare wheel is fitted. The car carries the official dating plate of the Veteran Car Club.

DRIVING A VETERAN

The 1901 Progress, at 180 guineas, was a typical low-priced car suitable for the owner-driver. The car tested was first owned by the master of the local work-house in Llandrindod Wells. The Progress is fitted with four-seater body-work; two of the passengers face the driver. Presumably this seat was de-signed for children; adults would se-verely restrict the driver's view. The car, built in Coventry, is fitted with a propri-etary single-cylinder motorcycle-type engine mounted at the rear, under the seat. A modern driver is immediately surprised by the upright steering column and confused by the four levers grouped around it! The original owner, however, might well have known no other layout. On the left of the wheel, the top lever selects the gears: pull back for low, push forward for high, and a notch between the two gives a neutral. Below is the ad-vance and retard lever for the ignition. On the right, a hand-throttle is the top lever; the other one controls inlet valve lift. There is one pedal on the floor – a footbrake which is only used in emer-gency, as it acts on the transmission. The handbrake, for ordinary use, is outside the car on the right; pushing the lever forward applies the brake.

To start the car, the petrol is turned on, the carburettor given a little tickle to get the fuel flowing, the ignition is retarded, the hand-throttle set for a medium to fast speed, the gear put in neutral, the inlet valve lever put on 'soft' tension, and the ignition turned on. The starting handle is inserted into a hole in the side of the bodywork and turned

25

ABOVE: *Looking vertically down on to the engine compartment under the rear seat of the 1901 Progress. The single cylinder engine is on the right, the gearbox on the left. The shafting and chains on the left are the mechanism for connecting the starting handle to the drive through the gearbox. The lever on the gearbox top is the gear change mechanism.*

LEFT: *The upright steering column with its four levers. Also shown is the single pedal for the rarely used transmission brake. To the right of the driver are the oil tank and its plunger, which is depressed approximately every 5 miles (8 km) to lubricate the principal parts of the engine. Originally this would have been a smaller bottle; this car has been modified to allow it to undertake the 50 mile (80 km) London to Brighton Run without replenishing the oil.*

over: with luck, the engine starts easily. If it is cold, the drag of cold oil in the gearbox makes cranking difficult.

To move off, the ignition is advanced, the valve pressure increased, the hand-brake pulled off and the gear slid gently towards the driver into low position. This is a clutch-and-gear combined operation, and take-off can be very smooth once the art of juggling it has been mastered. 10 to 12 miles (16-19 km) per hour is quite enough for low gear before high is selected — then the car seems to assume a lurching, galloping gait. In practice the

ABOVE: *The car is started by cranking at the side, a not uncommon practice on earlier veterans. When cranking any car, the thumb must be parallel with the fingers so that the hand can be thrown clear in the event of a backfire. Failure to do this often results in a broken arm or wrist.*

RIGHT: *The author at speed, around 25 miles (40 km) per hour; he is controlling the speed with the aid of the advance and retard lever in his left hand. Audible warning of approach is given by the bulb horn mounted on the right of the front seats.*

ABOVE: *A 1913 Fiat Tipo Zero. The hood gives more than adequate protection from the rain, though side screens would have given the complete closed car feel. The dickey seat (in single form the 'mother-in-law seat') looks very unsafe, judged by modern standards. A little step is provided by the rear mudguard for ease of entry to the dickey.*

BELOW: *The driving position seems very sparse compared to complicated modern cockpits. Floor pedals are conventional except that the accelerator is in the centre. The two gauges in front of the driver show pressure in the fuel tank and oil pressure. The button immediately above the clutch is a screw-in hand throttle and the one above that is the ignition cut-out. The Lucas switch panel and ammeter were added in 1917 when the car was converted to electrics.*

At speed in the Tipo Zero Fiat, the author is about to change gear from top to third. The large steering wheel is very prominent and the full-width windscreen provides good protection for the driver and passenger.

throttle and valve pressure can be set well forward and the speed controlled by the advance and retard lever. Very soon the driver will realise that he does not have enough hands; a change of direction and speed demands application of the hand-brake, movement of all four levers, and the turning of the steering wheel – hand signals tend to be forgotten at this time!

The steering is quite direct, and corners can be taken fairly quickly. The ride is smooth because of the more than adequate suspension – the sliding pillars on the front remind one of the Morgan, introduced eight years later. The handbrake is good by veteran standards, particularly in the dry; in the wet, the external contracting shoes get well lubricated with water.

It is easy to realise why early motorists had to dress up so well for every journey. On a winter's day it would be very chilly driving the Progress, and very wet in the rain!

By 1913 the typical owner-driver car could be a 1913 Fiat Tipo Zero, selling in standard form for £375. Now the car had a windscreen to protect the driver and passenger and a hood to cover them when it rained. Other passengers, usually children, could be carried in a dickey seat which folded out from the rear deck. Such passengers would have virtually no protection, and, if the hood were up, no forward visibility. The cockpit was roomy, but because of the outside gear lever and handbrake there was no driver's door. The spare wheel was also mounted on the offside running board. The Progress had no spare wheel, but by 1913 the detachable wheel was becoming general practice.

To start the car, first pump up pressure in the rear-mounted fuel tank with the cockpit-mounted hand pump, take off the retaining nut from the top of the carburettor, tickle the needle, set the hand throttle (just open) and turn on the ignition. The car is cranked from the front. If the engine is cold the choke is worked via a cable protruding through the radiator. Back in the cockpit the driver sees that, by modern standards, the pedals are almost conventional, only the accelerator being in a different position from today's, in the centre. The steering wheel appears very large. The four-speed gearbox, with a reverse, is a delight to use. The gears can be snicked through quickly, with appropriate double de-clutching, and a cruising speed of 35 to 40 miles (56-64 km) per hour is possible. On hills, you never run out of gears; you feel that it 'would climb up the side of a house' in low gear.

As produced, this basic family car had acetylene lights. The National Motor Museum's example, tested here, had its lights changed in 1917 for a set of Duco Electric lamps made and sold by the famous motor factors, Brown Brothers. A dynamo and battery were also added at this time.

The modern motorist driving the Fiat for the first time would realise that this was the ancestor of the car as we know it today — the Victorian Progress was 'primitive' by comparison.

POSTSCRIPT

Our Edwardian period finishes in 1918, the end of the Great War. Motor car production had stopped in Britain by 1916, so that year marks the true ending of this most delightful of all eras in motoring. During the war people were exhorted not to use their cars and those who did were often spat upon or shouted at. *The Times* and the *Daily Mail* carried very strong editorials against the use of the car. The disappearance of new British cars was partly met by imports from the United States, a country not as deeply involved in the war.

The First World War was the first fully mechanised war ever fought. Buses, lorries and almost every type of commercial vehicle were pressed into service. The Motor Volunteer Corps guaranteed to supply a certain number of private cars with drivers, and many officers took their civilian cars to the front with them. British industry very quickly switched over to producing the vehicles of war. Hundreds of people who had hardly come into contact with the motor vehicle before they volunteered or were called up were trained to be drivers or mechanics. These were to be the new car owners of the vintage period which followed.

Earl de la Warr was one of the people who took his own car with him when he went to serve in the First World War. Here you see him standing beside his Rolls-Royce Silver Ghost Landaulette built around 1914. Unusually, it is fitted with a windscreen for the chauffeur, or, in this case, Army driver.

Many people believe that the 'Prince Henry' Vauxhall which first appeared in 1910 was the first true British sports car. This 1913 example has typical two-seat accommodation, plus a dickey. The performance and road holding of this model were outstanding for the period. The sports car did not really develop until later on in the vintage period.

FURTHER READING

Over the years many books have been written that cover the subject of veteran cars, either in general terms or specific single makes. The following general books have been published in more recent times and should be available from either booksellers, good second-hand dealers or the public library. Any large autojumble will be attended by many specialist book dealers. Anyone contemplating research into any aspect of the veteran car will find the Library of the National Motor Museum at Beaulieu to be most helpful. The Library is open most weekdays but a prior appointment would be helpful (telephone: 01590 614652, email: malcolm.parsons@beaulieu.co.uk)

Baldwin, N.; Georgano, G. N.; Sedgwick, M.; Laban, B. *World Guide to Automobiles – The Makers and Their Marques.* Macdonald, 1987.
Bird, Anthony. *The Motor Car 1765–1914.* Batsford, 1960.
Bishop, G. *The Age of the Automobile.* Hamlyn, 1977.
Brendon, Piers. *The Motoring Centenary – The Story of the RAC.* Bloomsbury Press, 1997.
Burgess-Wise, D. *The Motor Car – An Illustrated International History.* Orbis, 1977.
Drackett, P., and Georgano, G. N. *The Encyclopedia of the Motor Car.* Octopus, 1979.
Flower, Raymond, and Wynn-Jones, Michael. *One Hundred Years of Motoring.* RAC, 1981.
Georgano, G. N. (editor). *The Beaulieu Encyclopedia of the Automobile.* The Stationery Office, 2000. Describes every make of veteran car.
Harper, Mark. *Mr Lionel – An Edwardian Episode.* Cassell, 1970.
History of the Motor Car. New English Library, 1971.
Hodges, D., and Burgess-Wise, D. *The Story of the Car.* Hamlyn, 1974.
Jeal, Malcolm (editor). *London to Brighton Run Centenary.* Veteran Car Cub, 1996.
Laux, James. *In First Gear – The French Automobile Industry.* Liverpool University Press, 1976.
Montagu of Beaulieu, Lord. *Antique Cars.* Golden Press, 1974.
Montagu of Beaulieu, Lord. *The Brighton Run.* Shire Publications, 1990.
Montagu of Beaulieu, Lord, and Bird, Anthony. *Steam Cars.* Cassell, 1971.
Montagu of Beaulieu, Lord, and McComb, F. Wilson. *Behind the Wheel.* Paddington Press, 1977.
Roberts, Peter. *A Pictorial History of the Automobile.* Grosset & Dunlap, 1977.
Sedgwick, Michael. *Veteran Cars.* Ward Lock, 1980.
Smith, Maurice (editor). *The Car.* St Michael, 1979.
Ware, Michael E. *The Making of the Motor Car.* Moorland, 1976.

There are many 'one-make' books that describe in detail the early models of that particular manufacturer.

MAGAZINES

Besides the magazine of the Veteran Car Club of Great Britain, there is no one publication that deals specifically with veteran cars. The following magazines, however, often carry articles on the subject: *The Automobile*, Enthusiast Publishing Limited, The Cottage Wood Manor, Seven Hills Road, Cobham, Surrey KT11 1ES (website: www.theautomobile.ndirect.co.uk) and *Classic and Sports Car*, Somerset House, Somerset Road, Teddington, Middlesex TW11 8RT (Haymarket Publishing, www.haymarketgroup.co.uk).

PLACES TO VISIT

There are many museums in Britain which have large collections of cars, but the following are known to have veteran cars and memorabilia and accessories of the period. An up-to-date listing of all road-transport museums in the United Kingdom can be found on www.motormuseums.com

Bentley Wildfowl and Motor Museum, Halland, Lewes, East Sussex BN8 5AF. Telephone: 01825 840573. Website: www.bentley.org.uk

C. M. Booth Collection of Historic Vehicles, 63-67 High Street, Rolvenden, near Cranbrook, Kent TN17 4LP. Telephone: 01580 241234.

Bradford Industrial Museum and Horses at Work, Moorside Mills, Moorside Road, Eccleshill, Bradford BD2 3HP. Telephone: 01274 631756. Website: www.bradford.gov.uk

Brooklands Museum, Brooklands Road, Weybridge, Surrey KT13 0QN. Telephone: 01932 857381. Website: www.brooklandsmuseum.com

Caister Castle Collection, Caister-on-Sea, Great Yarmouth, Norfolk NR30 5SN. Telephone: 01572 787251.

Grampian Transport Museum Trust, Alford, Aberdeenshire, Scotland AB33 8AE. Telephone: 01975 562292. Website: www.gtm.org.uk

Haynes Motor Museum, Sparkford, near Yeovil, Somerset BA22 7LH. Telephone: 01963 440804. Website: www.haynesmotormuseum.co.uk

Heritage Motor Centre, Banbury Road, Gaydon, Warwickshire CV35 0BJ. Telephone: 01926 641188. Website: www.heritage.org

Jaguar Daimler Heritage Trust, Jaguar Cars, Browns Lane, Allesley, Coventry, Warwickshire CV5 9DR. Telephone: 024 7640 2121.

Lakeland Motor Museum, Holker Hall and Gardens, Cark-in-Cartmel, Grange-over-Sands, Cumbria LA11 7PH. Telephone: 01539 558328. Website: www.holker-hall.co.uk

Leonardslee Gardens Veteran Car Museum, Lower Beeding, Horsham, West Sussex RH13 6PP. Telephone: 01403 891212.

Llangollen Motor Museum, Pentre Felin, Llangollen, Denbighshire LL20 8EE. Telephone: 01978 860324. Website: www.llangollenmotormuseum.co.uk

Museum of British Road Transport, Hales Street, Coventry, Warwickshire CV1 1PN. Telephone: 024 7683 2425. Website: www.mbrt.co.uk

Museum of Irish Transport, Scotts Gardens, Killarney, County Kerry, Ireland. Telephone: 00353 643 4677.

Museum of Science and Industry in Manchester, Liverpool Road, Castlefield, Manchester M3 4FP. Telephone: 0161 832 2244. Website: www.msim.org.uk

Museum of Transport, Kelvin Hall, 1 Bunhouse Road, Glasgow, Scotland G3 8DP. Telephone: 0141 287 2720.

National Motor Museum, John Montagu Building, Beaulieu, Brockenhurst, Hampshire SO42 7ZN. Telephone: 01590 612345. Website: www.beaulieu.co.uk

Sandringham House, Museum and Gardens, The Estate Office, Sandringham, Norfolk PE35 6EN. Telephone: 01553 772675. Website: www.sandringhamestate.co.uk

Science Museum Wroughton, Wroughton Airfield, Swindon, Wiltshire SN4 9NS. Telephone: 01793 814466. Website: www.sciencemuseum.org.uk/wroughton

Shuttleworth Collection, Old Warden Park, Biggleswade, Bedfordshire SG18 9EP. Telephone: 01767 627288. Website: www.shuttleworth.org

Skopos Motor Museum, Alexandra Mills, Alexandra Road, Batley, West Yorkshire WF17 6JA. Telephone: 01924 444423.

Streetlife – Hull Museum of Transport, High Street, Hull HU1 1PS. Telephone: 01482 613902. Website: www.hullcc.gov.uk

Ulster Folk and Transport Museum, Cultra, Holywood, County Down, Northern Ireland BT18 0EU. Telephone: 028 9042 8428.

MOTOR CLUBS

The only club in Britain that specifically caters for pre-1919 vehicles is the Veteran Car Club of Great Britain, Jessamine Court, 15 High Street, Ashwell, Hertfordshire SG7 5NL (telephone: 01462 742818; fax: 01462 742997; email: hq@vccofgb.co.uk; website: www.vccofgb.co.uk). There are many other single-make clubs that cater for owners of veteran cars of their particular make. There are many local old-car clubs that welcome owners of veteran cars. A list of such clubs can be obtained from the National Motor Museum at Beaulieu (email: malcolm.parsons@beaulieu.co.uk)